Getting Through the

Wilderness of Singleness

Jessica Davis

Getting Through the

Wilderness

of

Singleness

Copyright © 2014 by Jessica Davis

P.O. Box 1212 West Memphis, AR 72303 All Rights Reserved. Except as permitted under the U.S. copyright Act of 1976, no part of this publication may be reproduced, distributed, or transmitted in any form or by any means, or stored in a database or retrieval system, without the prior written permission of the publisher.

ISBN: 978-0-578-14392-7

Dedication

This book is dedicated to the memories of my grandparents, Bishop Frank & Elzeno Wells and Reverend Jesse & Sadie Selvy, Sr. You left fingerprints of grace in my life, and your legacy of life lessons will never be forgotten.

Acknowledgments

Apart from the efforts of me, the success of any vision depends largely on the encouragement and support of many others. I would like to take this opportunity to express my gratitude to the people who have been instrumental in the successful completion of this book. My greatest appreciation is to God for inspiring and trusting me with the gift of writing that He can use to bless others. OMG HUNNI, my husband, Jonathan Davis. I can't say thank you enough for your tremendous support and help. I feel motivated and encouraged every time I'm around you. Without your encouragement and guidance, this book would not have materialized. The passion and patience received from you was vital for the success of this book, and I am thankful for your untiring support and assistance. I love you baby!

Above all, I want to thank my parents, Mr. Jesse Selvy, Jr. and Mrs. Johnnie Selvy, and the rest of my family who supported and encouraged me to keep writing. You saw the gift and believed in me during this journey, and without you this book would have never found its way out of me and into the hands of so many wonderful people.

Last, but not least, I would like to express my gratitude to the many people who saw me through this book; to all those who provided support, talked things over, read, encouraged, offered comments, allowed me to share my testimony, assisted in the editing, proofreading, and design. Thank You and I Love You!

Contents

Dedication

Acknowledgments

Introduction — 2

Chapter One:
The Wilderness is for You — 5

Chapter Two:
It's Not Hard; It's a Choice — 9

Chapter Three:
Beware of Distractions — 18

Chapter Four: Confirmation — 23

Chapter Five: Preparation — 26

Chapter Six:
Plan of Salvation — 32

Chapter Seven:
So, When am I Ready for Marriage? — 38

Closing Prayer — 43

More Scriptures on Singleness — 45

References — 55

Getting Through the
Wilderness of Singleness

Getting Through the Wilderness of Singleness

Introduction

This book was inspired by God to encourage singles, which may be inquiring of God and even questioning, "Why Am I Not Married?" My mandate is to release insight that will inspire you as you prepare for Marriage Ministry in a

> *Single |sin•gle|*
> *(Verb)*
>
> *"Preparation While I Wait"*
> *Jessica Davis*

time and a season where SINGLENESS seems uncomfortable and unfair.

The Scriptures are full of principles and testimonies where God prepared His people before they obtained the blessing. One of the greatest models was the children of Israel's journey from Egypt to the Promise Land in the book Exodus. Moses delivered them out of bondage, but their failure to trust God in the Wilderness caused an eleven-day journey to be a forty-year cycle! Their negligence to God's plan gave way to a life of misery and death for all who thought the wilderness was a curse rather than a blessing.

This book is to express to you the necessity of "The Wilderness of Singleness!" My prayer is that you will be enlightened, strengthened, encouraged, and empowered to prepare as you wait.

"Singleness doesn't always feel good, but it's a place designed for your good."

And let us not lose heart and grow weary and faint in acting noble and doing right, for in due time and at the appointed season we shall reap, if we do not loosen and relax our courage and faint.

Galatians 6:9

Chapter

1

The Wilderness is for You

You may ask, "What does being Single have to do with the Wilderness? I'm alone, hurt, frustrated, tired, confused and left wondering will I ever reach that destination called Marriage?" Well, let me first encourage you by saying you are never alone. Yes, you may feel lonely at times, but in Matthew 28:20, Jesus said, "Surely I am with you always to the very end of the age."

> *Single is no longer a lack of options – but a choice.*
> *A choice to refuse to let your life be defined by your relationship status but to live every day Happily and let your Ever After work itself out.*
>
> *Mandy Hale*

Singleness is not a bad place, but a place designed for Detoxification and Preparation. The children of Israel were held captive by Egypt for over 400 years, according to Exodus 12:40-41. Although they knew that it wasn't a good place to be, they stayed and developed an immunity and tolerance for it!

Addicted to Unfruitful Relationships

I know what that feels like! At the age of eighteen, and fresh out of high school, I was in a relationship with a man that at the time, I didn't know was designed to destroy me. Much like Egypt, this relationship hurt me, used me, confused me, and had me feeling bitter and torn, but I just couldn't break away. I was addicted to an unfruitful relationship!

> *"I had struggled so hard and so long that I had simply exhausted myself, only to find that God had all the time in the world to wait for me to allow Him to free me."*
> Michelle McKinney

It is often very hard to end a love relationship even when you know it is bad for you. An "unfruitful" relationship is not the kind that goes through the usual periods of disagreement and disenchantment that are inevitable when two separate people come together. An unfruitful relationship is one that involves continual frustration. The relationship seems to have potential, but that potential is always just out of reach. In fact, the attachment in such relationships is to someone who is "unattainable", in the sense that he or she is committed to someone else, doesn't want a committed relationship, or is incapable of one. Unfruitful relationships are chronically lacking what God intends for you. Such relationships can destroy self-worth and prevent you from obtaining whom God truly has for you. Unfruitful relationships will mess you up mentally, physically, emotionally and spiritually! They are often fertile breeding grounds for loneliness, rage, and despair; therefore, remaining in a bad relationship will more than likely cause continual stress, wounds and scars.

After a while, for me, bondage no longer felt good! I cried out to God like the children of Israel did, and just as He sent Moses to deliver them out of bondage into a promised place, Jesus, my deliverer, led me out of that unfruitful relationship!

REALLY GOD? REALLY?

Out of bondage, but to their surprise, the next stop was the wilderness, a place intended for Detoxing and Preparing. (Deuteronomy 2:8) OMG! Six years in an Egypt situation and I finally got a way out. God, really? The Wilderness of Singleness? I go from having a man to no man at all! UGH! No dates, no hugs, no kisses, no gifts, no calls and no sex! Lord, what have you done to me, I cried? Just like the children of Israel, I began to feel like maybe Egypt was better for me. Have you ever been in a place where you felt like "A piece of a man is better than no man at all"? Even though you know the relationship is bad for you (and perhaps others have told you this), you crave it. Been there; done that!

I gave myself reasons to go back into the relationship that were not really accurate or that were not strong enough to counteract the ungodly aspects of the relationship. When I thought about being Single, I felt terrible anxiety and fear, which made me want to cling to it even more. Yes, I suffered painful withdrawal symptoms, including physical discomfort, which was only relieved by reestablishing contact. In a less obvious way I was reminded of the freedom to be truly loved by God's best, the freedom to love another person through choice rather than through dependency, and the freedom to leave a situation that is destructive (Proverbs 14:12).

REAL LOVE DOESN'T HURT!

Love is patient, love is kind. It does not envy, it does not boast, it is not proud. It does not dishonor others, it is not self-seeking, it is not easily angered, and it keeps no record of wrongs. Love does not delight in evil but rejoices with the truth. It always protects, always trusts, always hopes, and always preserves.

I Corinthians 13:4

Chapter

2

It's Not Hard; It's a Choice

If most of these signs apply to you, you are probably in an addictive, unfruitful relationship and have lost your will to allow God the right to direct your life. But I encourage you to move toward recovery, your first step must be to recognize that you are "hooked" and then try to understand the basis of your unfruitful relationship addiction. In this way, you gain the perspective to determine whether, in reality, the relationship can be improved or whether you need to leave it. I make an experienced plea to you; if it's not God ordained, it's not worth it!

> *"Singleness doesn't mean you don't have options – but you do have A Choice! A choice to refuse to let your life be defined by whether you're in a relationship but rather live every day "Happily" while GOD choose your "Ever After"*
>
> **Jessica Davis**

"What's to come is better than what's been". With that being said, Singleness is your time to allow God to cleanse you and purge you to rebuild you (Psalms 51:10-12).

"You're not ready for marriage yet because *Hurt people Hurt people*!" Think about it this way. Being married is about being the WOMAN you are meant to be, while being single allows you to focus on becoming the WIFE you were born to be!

Detoxification is a Must!

> ***"You cannot embrace the new without letting go of the old"***

But one thing I do, [it is my one aspiration]: forgetting what lies behind and straining forward to what lies ahead

Philippians 3:13b

Forgetting those things which are behind so you can reach forward to those things which are ahead can bring gut wrenching pain to your heart and make you feel as if there were a tug of war in your soul, threatening to tear you apart! But I'm here to tell you that you can forget those things which are behind and get to a place where you can remember them and/or see them without the pain and fear you felt while making the transition. Detoxification gives you the strength to press on toward this goal with exceeding joy.

Unfruitful relationships produce negative soul ties that are not easily broken. Detoxification is a period of mental, physical, emotional and spiritual treatment which consists of prayer, fasting, reading the Word of God, seeking wise counsel, and staying busy caring for the things of The Lord according to 1 Corinthians 7:34. This process helps you overcome physical and psychological dependence on someone and/or something other than Christ.

> **It all starts in the mind!**
>
> *Do not conform to the pattern of this world, but be transformed by the renewing of your mind. Then you will be able to test and approve what God's will is—his good, pleasing and perfect will.*
>
> ***ROMANS 12:2***

Step One: Cutting Soul Ties

A soul tie is a linkage in the soul realm between two people. It links their souls together, which can bring forth both beneficial results and negative results.
The positive effect of a soul tie: In a godly marriage, God links the two together, and the Bible tells us that they become one flesh. As a result of them becoming one flesh, it binds them together and they will cleave onto one

another in a unique way. The purpose of this cleaving is to build a very healthy, strong, and close relationship between a man and a woman.

> **MATTHEW 19:5,** *"And said, for this cause shall a man leave father and mother, and shall cleave to his wife: and they twain shall be one flesh."*

If in fact you've engaged in a sexual relationship with a partner before marriage, **YOU ARE NOT SINGLE**, and must cut those ties first before cleaving to your husband/wife.
Ungodly Soul ties are used to the devil's advantage. Soul ties formed from sex outside of marriage causes a person to become defiled.

> **GENESIS 34:2-3,** *"And when Shechem the son of Hamor the Hivite, prince of the country, saw her, he took her, and lay with her, and defiled her. And his soul cleaved unto Dinah the daughter of Jacob, and he loved the damsel, and spoke kindly unto the damsel."*

This is why it is so common for a person to still have 'feelings' towards an ex-lover that they have no right to be attracted to in that way. Twenty years down the road, a person may still think of their first lover or sexual partners, even if he or she has moved on with a new partner. This is all because of a soul tie!

Demonic spirits can also take advantage of ungodly soul ties and use them to transfer spirits between one person to another. Most ungodly relationships cannot just be severed without deliverance. Spirits are real and will keep you bound and chained. Soul ties are unhealthy and can keep you in the wilderness longer than expected, take you further than expected, and cause you to pay a price not expected! They are just the remains of your unsaved self, which God does not want you to carry into your destiny for the fact that it holds the potential to pull you back from what God has called you into. All it takes is just one sniff, one touch, one taste of that ungodly tie; it can hold you bound from what God has for you. If you're reading this, it is because God loves you and wants to break you out of anything that can stop you from your destiny in God.

Step Two: Deliverance

When you have an ungodly soul tie, you need deliverance because it makes you vulnerable to manipulation and it takes the place of God in your life. It is important that you first identify where you have opened the window for the enemy to enter into your life. Surrender your life to Jesus and let him rule over your soul. If there have been any covenants made by words or action, take some time out to pray, and one, by one in the name of Jesus, begin to denounce all the contacts you have made.

Denounce the soul ties by confessing it out loud and accept the blood of Christ to wash your sins away. Shut every door of fear with the word of God and claim the promises of God. Now, make it a point to fill your mind with the things of God instead. Throw away everything that reminds you of your past. Stay tuned to the Holy Spirit and walk in the presence of God. If this struggle still persists, you might need help from your spiritual leader. Take time to open up about your struggle with him/her and seek help.

Personal Deliverance Prayer:
Father, I know you love me. Forgive me for every soul tie I have developed. (Name them out) with (person or persons) that would affect me adversely. I surrender myself into Your Hands and ask that you would establish Your Lordship in my life. In Jesus' name, I renounce and break every authority I've given to this relationship, and I break this soul tie in Jesus' name and set myself free. Thank you. Amen.

Step Three: Me, Myself, & God

A busy, vibrant, goal-oriented single Christian is much more attractive than someone who waits around for anyone other than God to validate his/her existence.
Mandy Hale

After true deliverance from soul ties due to unfruitful relationships: staying busy is very vital to stay free (Galatians 5:1-2). Getting busy is the most basic thing we need to do in order to stay focused on what's to come. Your relationship with God is the goal of Christianity and where the true joy in being a Single Christian is found. So if you neglect it, you're missing the whole point of the wilderness.

Spending time with God is fun. That doesn't mean it's always easy, but once you establish a relationship with Him, He then teaches you how to love and be loved.

I found that my time with Him was, and is, the highlight of my day.

You can relate to God just as you would a close friend. While this may be a hard concept to grasp at first, in time you will experience what it means to have God as your friend. Jesus made His time with God a priority (read the stories in Mark 25, Luke 22:39, and Luke 5:16) and set the example for how we are to relate to our heavenly Father.

There are many reasons to discipline ourselves to spend time with God. Here are some of the things that happen when we are close to Him:

- **You can more easily find out what God wants for your life**
- **You can refocus and get your mind off the world and worries around you**

- **He rebuilds you as you worship Him**
- **You naturally & spiritually become more like Him**
- **The more time you spend with God, the more your value increases because**

Through Reading the Bible, Prayer, and Worship, He teaches you what real love is, how to receive it, and redistribute it.

Need Help Getting Started?

Spending time with God is not difficult. In many ways, spending time with God is a bit like exercising. Many people find that when they begin an exercise program, the "fun" stage quickly wears off and it requires a lot of discipline to keep at it. But for those who do stick with it through this tough time, exercising regularly becomes fun, comes easy, and they can't imagine wanting to go without it.

So if you're still working to make time with God a part of your life, keep at it. Like any lifetime habit, set reasonable goals that you can maintain for a long period of time and slowly increase the time you spend with God as you mature in your faith. When the "fun stage" wears off, as it likely will, ask God to help you stick with it. He wants this time with you and will give you the desire and discipline to make it through. The difficult times don't last forever, and soon you will find that your daily time with God is something you wouldn't even think of missing. So then, the next time you're hit with the age-old question "Why are you still single?" be mature enough to boldly say,**"BECAUSE I'M TOO VALUABLE TO SETTLE!"**

Chapter

3

Beware of Distractions

> *And I am certain that God, who began the good work within you, will continue his work until it is finally finished on the day when Christ Jesus returns.*
> ***PHILLIPIANS 1:6***

Distractions come to take your full attention off of God. Therefore, getting involved as much as you can is necessary. You may set your attention and time to volunteer in the community, church activities, mission trips, Christian organizations, work, school, gym and etc., because an idle mind is a dangerous mind! (Philippians 4:8)

Flirting with distractions will cause you to become an enemy of God and His way. Please don't suppose that God doesn't care. The proverb has it that "He's a fiercely jealous lover", and what He gives in love is far better than anything else you'll find. It's common knowledge that "God goes against the willful proud; God gives grace to the willing humble." So let God work His will in you. Yell a loud no to the Devil and watch him scamper. Say a quiet yes to God and He'll be there in no time. Don't spend time dabbling in sin! Keep your inner man purified. The enemy's job is to distract you with opportunities to play the field (I Corinthians 10:13). If you so happen to fall, get up quickly and declare to the devil, "The fun and games are over." Get serious, really serious. Get down on your knees before the Master and repent because it's the only way you'll get on your feet (James 4:4-10).

Seasons of Frustration

Marriage was something that I wanted more than anything else in the entire world, yet it was not coming my way. I even convinced myself that the reason I wanted it was so I could please God. One day, in a moment of frustration, I cried out, "Why won't you let me do your will?" In a still, small voice, the Spirit responded, "You don't want to do my will. You want me to do yours. You're NOT ready yet." OMG, this hit me hard! I knew that what He was saying was true and that I had to make the choice between getting what I wanted and letting God give me what He wanted. After a few months of struggle:
- No One
- The Wrong One
- The Married One
- The Almost Perfect One

I opened my hand and let go of what I had so desperately been trying to grasp. I prayed, "Lord, if You never give to me what I have been asking for, that's okay. You have already blessed me with more than I deserve. I will be content with what you think is best for me." Months passed and then suddenly, when I least expected it, God gave me what I had been praying for; I met Jonathan. It was not because I had been trying to twist His arm, but it was because I was finally ready to receive love with the right motive! During the dark and lonely nights when there was no one to go out with and friends were busy, I reminded myself that God is a good God and He will withhold no good thing from me. My part: obey the Bible, trust my Lord, and fall in love with Him first and foremost. This helped me refocus my attitude and get my mind off a man and on God.

How Do I Know He's the One?

It's okay to be careful when you think God has given you something. If He has really given it to you, and you are yielded and obedient to His Word in every way possible, then He will be the one who will bring it about. You do not have to force it to take place. He always does it in a miraculous way that it will give Him glory and honor every time, and watching Him work in your own personal life is the most exciting thing you will ever experience. Even if, at first, a person resists what God has told them, it is their obedience to the word, The Holy Bible, and humility toward God that allows Him to move in the way He wants for them. You will know he/she is the one because everything God speaks must line up with His Holy Bible in every way, or it is not from Him. God never contradicts His own Word. That is why it is so important to know the scriptures. If a person's thoughts and actions are not yielded to the Word, and they don't line up correctly, it could be a trap of Satan to tempt you into something wrong or an idea from their own desires of the sinful nature, which we are all born with (Romans 7:25). Thanks be to God-through Jesus Christ our Lord! So then, I am a slave to God's law, but in the sinful nature a slave to the law of sin. Read in Paul's writings about the power of our sinful nature and how it tries to have control over a person's actions, which will keep them out of God's perfect will (Romans 7:8-14).

ASK YOURSELF

-Will this relationship bring glory to God and to Jesus?
-Would Jesus stand beside us the whole time, or would any part of this make Him back away?
-Is this in the best interest for everyone involved?
-What will be written on my record in heaven?

Take the time to check to see if God's Fruit of the Spirit is in his/her thoughts and actions. Check to see if they are visible in any actions that are involved with what you are thinking of doing. These are supernatural fruit in a person's life that are produced by God and His Holy Spirit working in their mind and heart; they go beyond the fruit that are humanly produced, and there is never any corruption where the Fruit of the Spirit exists. (Galatians 5:22-23) But the fruit of the Spirit is love, joy, peace, patience, kindness, goodness, faithfulness, gentleness and self-control. Marriage is a good thing, but it is worth the wait. The old adage is that it is better to be single than in a bad marriage. I agree with that. I will also add that marriage is hard enough when you are confident that you married someone the Lord led you to. Marriage is not worth jumping into unless you are ready and have the right one.

Chapter

4

Confirmation

The Holy Spirit will help you to come to the right conclusions, so be patient and wait upon the Lord. Ask God for confirmation any time you are unsure of the thoughts in your mind about a person. The human mind is the playground for Satan's works. Learn to put him to flight. It's so simple. All Christians have authority over Satan. He does his best to keep us from knowing it. If we do know about it, then he lies and intimidates us to keep us from using it. Examine what's going on in your mind and your actions after connecting with this person to find out whether they are Godly or Ungodly; negative or positive; bound or free! The Bible is our measuring stick for comparison. The closer to God you are, through knowing the Word and applying obedience, the more you will know. Satan has been cursed from the moment he was thrown out of heaven. Anything he does or tries to do to people is a curse. We are not to allow anything in the curse to enter into our lives. Fight the good fight of faith to keep it out (Galatians 3:13).

Jesus paid the price for us to be free from all the wrong and sinful influences that Satan tries to push into all areas of our lives, physically, mentally, emotionally, and spiritually; remember, you have been set free!!

What Do I do if He's Not the One?

Once more, don't get connected to them in any deep relationship. Fulfill the obligation of the Fruit of the Spirit and try to win them for the Lord, but don't become ensnared in their lifestyle.

2 Timothy 2:23-26 says, don't have anything to do with foolish and stupid arguments, because you know they produce quarrels. And the Lord's servant must not quarrel; instead, he must be kind to everyone, able to teach, not resentful. Those who oppose him he must gently instruct, in the hope that God will grant them repentance leading them to a knowledge of the truth, and that they will come to their senses and escape from the trap of the devil, who has taken them captive to do his will. Before entering into a relationship with him/her check for these characteristics.
(2 Timothy 3:1-5) But mark this: There will be terrible times in the last days. People will be lovers of themselves, lovers of money, boastful, proud, abusive, disobedient to their parents, ungrateful, unholy, without love, unforgiving,

> *Trust in the LORD with all your heart and lean not on your own understanding; in all your ways submit to him, and he will direct your path.*
> *PROVERBS 3:5-6*

slanderous, without self-control, brutal, not lovers of the good, treacherous, rash, conceited, lovers of pleasure rather than lovers of God-- having a form of godliness but denying its power. Have nothing to do with them.
Since the human mind is the place that Satan works you must test the spirit that is producing thoughts in your mind (1 John 4:1-3).

Dear friends, do not believe every spirit, but test the spirits to see whether they are from God, because many false prophets have gone out into the world. This is how you can recognize the Spirit of God: Every spirit that acknowledges that Jesus Christ has come in the flesh is from God, but every spirit that does not acknowledge Jesus is not from God. This is the spirit of the Antichrist, which you have heard is coming and even now is already in the world (2 Corinthians 6:14).

If you pray first and ask God to show you His truth, and let Jesus know that your trust is completely in Him, I assure you that your answer will come quickly. The authority that was given to us by Christ gives every born again Christian the right to demand an answer. If he or she is from Satan your confirmation answer will always be no. You can then rebuke Satan and order him to leave your thoughts alone. However, God's spirit will gladly confirm, "yes" if he or she is the one. You are then free to ask the Lord to align your thoughts with the Bible and His way of doing things.

Chapter

5

Preparation

For most of my young adult life, I remember desiring a husband. I did not meet my husband until I was 28 years old, so I spent half of my life praying, waiting, and preparing. My desire for marriage was intense. It was one of my top prayer requests. As a Bible believing Christian, I had to combat the loneliness with faith. God promised in His Word that if He was willing to give me Jesus, who was the greatest gift, I could trust Him for other things, like a husband. So then the preparation began.

God reminded me that in the midst of waiting and hoping, I had at my disposal the sovereignty of God, who would even use angels to help with my love life, and the instrument of prayer, where I could ask Him for help. Our relationship began to teach me that I had more to work on than just my appearance, personality, and wedding plans! Marriage is much more than that. Yes, you guessed it right; Marriage is Ministry!

Marriage is the act of serving one another. You can believe it. You do serve in your marriage, and therefore, it is a ministry. You and your spouse being ministers has nothing to do with serving one another. The fact is, your service to your spouse is actually an act of service unto God (Ephesians 5:21-33).

Loving and serving God with all your heart, soul and might is the exercising of vows you promised to keep in His presence to your spouse (Luke 10:27).
Every time you worship, praise, obey, submit, communicate (pray), and repent to God in your Wilderness of Singleness, you are positioning yourself to serve your spouse in the same manner. Listening to them when they want to talk, complimenting, supporting them in their dreams, careers and/or visions, and saying I'm sorry are just a few examples of serving the Lord that will be productive in your marriage.

Intimacy preparation with God is needful, fun and rewarding both naturally and spiritually. This allows closeness and openness between husband and wife that strengthens the relationship and establishes trust in every area. Yes, trusting your spouse makes it much easier to cleave to one another (Genesis 2:24).

On the other hand, distrust is a breeding ground for fear, worry, doubt, and disbelief, which affects vital nutrients that are needed for a healthy marriage. God expects well-balanced marriages to be models for other couples and singles that want to get married.

Love and commitment to God first, and your spouse secondly is expected in order to minister to others in a positive, not negative way! That's why preparation is necessary. It gets you ready to handle your promised place, and hopefully once you get there, your actions are positive and others will see what a healthy marriage looks like. Preparation makes certain that you are equipped with respect and love that will be seen by family, friends, and even strangers. Most importantly, your children will be a carbon copy of your marriage. The way you serve in your relationship with God and your spouse sets the standard for your children when they become adults and start their lives of service (2 Corinthians 3:1-3).

Marriage ministry wasn't meant to be trivial nor unobtainable. However, you must be willing to allow God the time He needs to prep you for it! As He does His part and you do yours, your marriage will remain strong and bring satisfaction and enjoyment.

The whole Wilderness process is to equip you for the long haul, a place where God teaches you discipline and stability. According to Proverbs 2:18-22, marriage is an irrevocable covenant/contract to which we are bound. Therefore, when two people get married, they PROMISE that they will be faithful to each other regardless of what happens. The children of Israel changed places, but God didn't change His position, nor the promise! He expects us to stay in His will, no matter what oppositions arise in our marriage.

As a wife, you must be prepared to promise that you will be faithful to your husband, even if he is afflicted with BULGES, BALDNESS, BUNIONS, and BIFOCALS, or even if someone more exciting comes along. The husband must also be prepared to promise to be faithful, even if the wife loses her BEAUTY and APPEAL, if she is not as NEAT and TIDY or as SUBMISSIVE as he would like her to be, if she is sickly, or if she spends more MONEY than she should. She may even be a TERRIBLE COOK! Your time in the Wilderness of Singleness is designed to teach you how to illuminate the positive and be thankful for who God has ordained as yours. I believe time spent murmuring, grumbling, and complaining about your wilderness process are signs of an ungrateful nagging spouse who is not ready to be married.

> *Marriage is a total commitment and a total sharing of the total person with your spouse until death.*

You can't do this with an Egypt mentality. God's way is that by the time you're ready for marriage, you will be ready to share everything – your body, your possessions, your insights, your ideas, your abilities, your problems, your successes, your sufferings, your failures, and so on. God plus husband and wife equals a team, and whatever either one does, they do it for the good of the other. Being concerned about the other person's needs instead of your own needs is a sign of maturity.

Marriage is about becoming one flesh, but this one flesh must manifest itself in practical, tangible, demonstrable ways that I learned while going through my Wilderness of Singleness.

- **In the same way, husbands ought to love their wives as they love their own bodies (Ephesians 5:28).**
- **Her husband has full confidence in her and lacks nothing of value. She brings him well, not harm, all the days of her life (Proverbs 31:11-12).**
- **She carefully watches everything in her household and suffers nothing from laziness (Proverbs 31:27).**

Proper preparation is not intended to be in theory only, but a concrete reality. Total deliverance, healing, restoration and preparation are all part of God's blueprint for a good marriage. In the Wilderness of Singleness, He breaks down barriers, destroys walls that divide, cleanses our sin, breaks the power of reigning sin, sets the mind free, and gives us the power of the Holy Spirit, who produces in you the fruit of love, joy, peace, patience, kindness, goodness, faithfulness, gentleness, and self-control that will last a lifetime. So remember, God's will for you is to Leave & Let

Go of Egypt, Cleave to Him 1st, and Prepare Yourself to Receive WHO and WHAT He has promised you!

The following are some verses that helped me through the hard and lonely days of being single.
(All scripture references will be from the New International Version of the Bible)

1.) Romans 8:32, "He who did not spare his own Son, but gave him up for us all-- how will he not also, along with him, graciously give us all things?"

2.) Genesis 24:7, 12, "He will send his angel before you so that you can get a wife for my son from there . . .. Then he prayed, "O LORD, God of my master Abraham, give me success today, and show kindness to my master Abraham."

3.) Proverbs 19:14, "Houses and wealth are inherited from parents, but a prudent wife is from the LORD."

4.) Song of Solomon 2:7 "Do not arouse or awaken love until it so desires."

5.) Psalm 84:11, "No good thing does he withhold from those whose walk is blameless."

I pray that upon reading this book, you are inspired to view the Wilderness of Singleness experience as a necessary place that allows God a chance to prepare you for "Total Oneness" before you get married. Marriage is a spiritual union, so if you are not saved, you need to come to Jesus Christ. But how do you do that?

Chapter

6

Plan of Salvation

According to the Word of God, it is very simple to be saved and takes only a second to explain.

Man Was Born a Sinner
Isaiah 53:6, "All we like sheep have gone astray; we have turned everyone to his own way; and the LORD hath laid on him the iniquity of us all."
John 3:3, "Jesus answered and said unto him, Verily, verily, I say unto thee, Except a man be born again, he cannot see the kingdom of God."
Romans 3:10, "As it is written, There is none righteous, no, not one."
Romans 3:23, "For all have sinned, and come short of the glory of God."
There is a price on our sin—eternal death in Hell.
Romans 6:23, "For the wages of sin is death; but the gift of God is eternal life through Jesus Christ our Lord."
Romans 5:12, "Wherefore, as by one man sin entered into

the world, and death by sin; and so death passed upon all men, for that all have sinned."
2 Thessalonians 1:8, "In flaming fire taking vengeance on them that know not God, and that obey not the gospel of our Lord Jesus Christ."
Revelation 20:15, "And whosoever was not found written in the book of life was cast into the lake of fire."
Revelation 21:8, "But the fearful, and unbelieving, and the abominable, and murderers, and whoremongers, and sorcerers, and idolaters, and all liars, shall have their part in the lake which burneth with fire and brimstone: which is the second death."

Jesus paid that price by dying on the cross and shedding His blood; Christ was buried and rose again!

Romans 5:8, "But God commended his love toward us, in that, while we were yet sinners, Christ died for us."
John 3:16, "For God so loved the world, that he gave his only begotten Son, that whosoever believeth in him should not perish, but has everlasting life."
1st Timothy 1:15, "This is a faithful saying, and worthy of all acceptation, that Christ Jesus came into the world to save sinners; of whom I am chief."
1st Peter 1:18-19, "Forasmuch as ye know that ye were not redeemed with corruptible things, as silver and gold, from your vain conversation received by tradition from your

fathers; But with the precious blood of Christ..."
1st Corinthians 15:1-4, "Moreover, brethren, I declare unto you the gospel which I preached unto you, which also ye have received, and wherein ye stand; By which also ye are saved, if ye keep in memory what I preached unto you, unless ye have believed in vain. For I delivered unto you first of all that which I also received, how that Christ died for our sins according to the scriptures; And that he was buried, and that he rose again the third day according to the scriptures." By faith in Jesus Christ ALONE we can be saved.

Salvation is NOT found in a religion or good works, but in a Person... The LORD JESUS CHRIST!

John 11:25, "Jesus said unto her, I am the resurrection, and the life: he that believeth in me, though he was dead, yet shall he live."

John 14:6, "Jesus saith unto him, I am the way, the truth, and the life: no man cometh unto the Father, but by me."

John 6:40, "And this is the will of him that sent me, that everyone which seeth the Son, and believeth on him, may have everlasting life: and I will raise him up at the last day."

Mark 1:15, "And saying, the time is fulfilled, and the kingdom of God is at hand: repent ye, and believe the gospel."

Acts 26:18, "To open their eyes, and to turn them from darkness to light, and from the power of Satan unto God, that they may receive forgiveness of sins, and inheritance among them, which are sanctified by faith that is in me."

Romans 10:13, "For whosoever shall call upon the name of the Lord shall be saved."

1 Corinthians 3:11, "For other foundation can no man lay than that is laid, which is Jesus Christ."

Galatians 3:26, "For ye are all the children of God by faith in Christ Jesus."

Jesus has already done His part, now you must do yours! Do you admit that you are a GUILTY sinner, under the condemnation of God's LAW, deserving of Hellfire?

Do you believe that Jesus is the Son of God (God in the flesh) who died upon the cross, sacrificing His precious blood to pay for your sins? Do you believe that Jesus was buried and rose again three days later?

That is the good news of the gospel... Jesus DIED, He was BURIED, and He is RISEN! If you would like to be saved, simply come in your heart as a guilty sinner and BELIEVE upon the Lord Jesus Christ.

Now Say This Prayer:

Dear Jesus,
I admit that I am a sinner deserving of Hell. I believe that you died, were buried and rose again. Please forgive me of my sins and take me to Heaven when I die. I now believe upon you alone, apart from all self-righteous works and religion, as my personal Savior. Thank you, Amen.

Just as you were born physically to your parents, so were you born spiritually into the Family of God when you received Jesus! Please understand that we are not saved because we pray a prayer, but because we believe upon the Lord Jesus Christ. It is certainly appropriate to ask the Lord in prayer to forgive and save us, but it is our faith that prompts us to pray. Salvation is of the heart, as we read in Romans 10:10, "For with the heart man believeth unto righteousness…"

Your faith just SAVED you! There is NO self-righteousness involved in salvation. It is the gift of God. You see, we have no righteousness of our own to offer God. No amount of good can undo the bad we've done. Thus, Jesus paid a debt that He did not owe, because we owed a debt that we could not pay. Salvation is receiving, not giving. We are Sinners and Jesus is the Savior. Jesus loves "YOU" just that much!

HALLELUJAH, YOU ARE SAVED

Just take God at His word and claim His salvation by faith. You say, "Surely, it cannot be that simple!" Yes, that simple. It is scriptural; it is God's plan. My friend, believe on Jesus and receive Him as your personal Savior!! Romans 8:34, "Who is he that condemneth? It is Christ that died, yea rather, that is risen again, who is even at the right hand of God, who also maketh intercession for us."

Chapter

7

<u>So, When am I Ready for Marriage?</u>

You are ready when you're no longer a child and when you're ready to take on the adult responsibilities that marriage brings. Paul stated, "When I was a child, I spoke and thought and reasoned as a child. But when I grew up, I put away childish things (1 Corinthians 13:11)." When we think about "maturity", there are different ways in which people can be mature and different ways in which they can be immature. It is possible for an emotional dwarf to look like a physical giant as well as a grown man to be as immature as a 10-year-old boy. The same as a beautiful woman to be an emotional child. Please don't be fooled by age or statue. Marriage requires maturity--point blank!

I've seen immaturity in marriage cause many marriages to fail. Because most adults never outgrow childhood immaturity, they demonstrate it in their marriage. It doesn't take much insight to see those areas of immaturity in you or mate, but failure to make changes makes problems in the marriage inevitable. Immaturity produces major problems in marriage, no matter how handsome, beautiful, or sexy the man and/or woman may be. Maturity means more than the desire to get married, the ability to conceive children, and the ability to earn enough money to live on.

Some people do get married immature and the marriage somehow survives until maturity is developed, but the best time to develop the maturity needed for marriage is before marriage, not after marriage. The kind of maturity needed for marriage is in God's Word. If you are not mature enough to be married and you want to be mature when you marry, make the Bible your guidebook. What you need for marriage is the kind of maturity that enables you to fulfill your commitments until the hardship is over, or even if it is never over (Psalms 15:4). Godly principles leave no room for excuses!

The "I'm Just Not Ready" Excuse

Come on now, how long will you keep up this foolery? This half-truth has been just a means of dodging the responsibility of marriage. Everyone desires companionship unless you're specially gifted for celibacy. "Nope, not my ministry!" Contrary to popular belief, I believe Christian men and women should be moving in the direction of marriage between ages 18 and 30. This is not only the best time for meeting mates, but also the most fertile time for forming families. However, if you don't feel like you're ready to take on being married, the solution certainly isn't wandering around the Wilderness from one relationship to another!

I believe, based on what I have read in Scripture, that believers are called either to celibacy or marriage (Matthew 19:11-12). You have to pray and ask God which status applies to you. I knew from my desires and drives for companionship that I was not graced with the gift of celibacy, No Sir-Re-Bob! God revealed to me that I was indeed called to be an ordained wife. God, with his infinite wisdom, taught me how to handle the responsibilities that came with marriage ministry while yet being single!

I knew I was close to being married because I would pray and study every day that God would make me a godly wife as I positioned myself for a godly husband. I knew I needed more than lips, hips, and fingertips, so I began asking for wisdom and knowledge in the areas of:

- **Cooking:** A Virtuous Woman cares for her body. She prepares healthy food for her family (Proverbs 31: 14 – 15, Proverbs 31: 17).
- **Cleaning:** A Virtuous Woman is a homemaker. She creates an inviting atmosphere of warmth and love for her family and guests. She uses hospitality to minister to those around her (Proverbs 31: 15, Proverbs 31: 20 – 22, Proverbs 31: 27).
- **Beauty:** A Virtuous Woman is a woman of worth and beauty. She has the inner beauty that only comes from Christ. She uses her creativity and sense of style to create beauty in her life and the lives of her loved ones (Proverbs 31: 10 Proverbs 31: 21 – 22, Proverbs 31:24-25).
- **Serving:** A Virtuous Woman respects her husband. She does him well all the days of her life. She is trustworthy and a helpmeet (Proverbs 31: 11- 12, Proverbs 31: 23, Proverbs 31: 28).
- **Timing:** A Virtuous Woman uses her time wisely. She works diligently to complete her daily tasks. She does not spend time dwelling on those things that do not please the Lord (Proverbs 31: 13, Proverbs 31: 19, Proverbs 31: 27, Proverbs 16: 9).
- **Budgeting:** A Virtuous Woman seeks her husband's approval before making purchases and spends money wisely. She is careful to purchase quality items, which her

family needs (Proverbs 31: 14, Proverbs 31: 16, Proverbs 31: 18).

• **Balancing:** A Virtuous Woman serves her husband, her family, her friends, and her neighbors with a gentle and loving spirit. She is charitable (Proverbs 31: 12, Proverbs 31: 15, Proverbs 31: 20).

By this time, it had become more than just seeking out companionship. The challenge was being the "best that I could be" in every area of my life. Proverbs 31 gave me hope and challenged me to come up. For single men who are looking for an honorable wife, it is a biblical model of a godly woman. This scripture begins by stating that an excellent wife is difficult to find, but when she is found, "she is far more precious than jewels" (Proverbs 31:10). It appears that the Proverbs 31 woman spent her days in the "Wilderness of Singleness" preparing herself for doing good unto others, starting with herself. She was a woman of character who could be trusted as a wife! She gives the challenge to rise above the bar and the hope that through God's grace, a woman can live a life that brings glory to her Lord and becomes a blessing to her household.

A Confident Woman is Complete

Complete: [kəm/'plēt] to make whole or perfect (mature).

Confidence says, "I know who I am and whose I am. I can give love and receive love genuinely without fear, shame, and intimidation. I'm not bound by my past, neither by what others think, say or feel about me. I don't have to fake it till I make it. I know what I want and where I'm going because I've been with God!"

God caused Adam to fall asleep at Eve's creation, and it was only after she was complete that God caused Adam to awake and He brought the two together. Both Adam and Eve were formed, worked on, and completed by God when they met. The ministry of marriage was meant to "compliment" each other rather than complete each other! I think it's safe to say that getting rid of unfruitful baggage is a great way to give the very best of yourself to your spouse without restraints. Your focus should be on loving him or her in the best and healthiest way that you can. Don't get me wrong, there will still be several areas that God needs to work on in your life after marriage, however, there should be a definite change and growing inside of you as you follow God!

Be encouraged friend. You are a constant work in progress and won't ever be literally perfect on this side of heaven. God is the only one who can determine whether you're ready for marriage, and ultimately ready to give your spouse "your best." So until HE speaks, keep desiring to grow in every area of your life — for your lover, for yourself, and of course, for your Lord!

Closing Prayer

"Lord God, Your Word declares that if I delight myself in you and enjoy and seek your pleasure above mine, that You'd give me the desires of my heart (Psalm 37:4). Desiring a husband/wife is neither evil nor selfish because marriage is honorable according to Hebrews 13:4. At the beginning of creation, You proclaimed, "It is not good that man should be alone" and then You created Eve to be a suitable partner for Adam in Genesis 2:18.

In the name of Jesus, I ask that You would protect the husband/wife, a suitable partner—You have chosen for me and because the covenant of marriage is sacred according to Mark 10:9, I ask for a man/woman of God.

Please give me a husband/wife whose love for me is only outmatched by his/her love for You; a man/woman who will cherish me and build me up naturally and spiritually; a man/woman who will honor me according to I Peter 3:7 and our marriage vows; a man/woman who will be a good father/mother; lover and friend; a man/woman whom I will be attracted to physically, emotionally, and spiritually; a soul mate who will love me as Christ loves me.

Keep me from attaching myself to another man/woman out of desperation. I will not settle for a relationship that's second best, convenient, or one that feeds my insecurities. Guard my purity and give me the patience to wait. And when I meet him/her, confirm to me that he/she is the one.

Release from me the baggage of past relationships, and

prepare me for the man/woman you have chosen to be my husband/wife. Free me from any hindrances to a healthy and godly marriage: insecurities, habitual sins, selfishness, and emotional hurt. Dispel my unrealistic expectations that set me up for disappointment.

I place my trust in You, rather than my partner. In this period of waiting, I will look to You, alone, to be my companion and best friend. You are the one who redeems my life from the pit, who crowns me with love and compassion, who satisfies my desires with good things according to Psalm 103:4-5, and I will not be anxious. But as I present my requests to You, flood me with the peace that surpasses all understanding so that my heart and my mind are guarded in Christ Jesus according to Philippians 4:6, 7.

In this request, I commit myself to trust you and do well, as I dwell in the Wilderness of Singleness and feed on your faithfulness. I commit my way to You and trust that You will bring it to pass according to Psalm 37:35. In the name of Jesus, Amen!

More Scriptures on Singleness

1 Corinthians 7:32-35

I want you to be free from anxieties. The unmarried man is anxious about the things of the Lord, how to please the Lord. But the married man is anxious about worldly things, how to please his wife, and his interests are divided. And the unmarried or betrothed woman is anxious about the things of the Lord, how to be holy in body and spirit. But the married woman is anxious about worldly things, how to please her husband. I say this for your own benefit, not to lay any restraint upon you, but to promote good order and to secure your undivided devotion to the Lord.

2 Corinthians 6:14

Do not be unequally yoked with unbelievers. For what partnership has righteousness with lawlessness? Or what fellowship has light with darkness?

1 Corinthians 7:1-40

Now concerning the matters about which you wrote: "It is good for a man not to have sexual relations with a woman." But because of the temptation to sexual immorality, each man should have his own wife and each woman her own husband. The husband should give to his wife her conjugal rights, and likewise the wife to her husband. For the wife does not have authority over her own body, but the husband does. Likewise the husband does not have authority over his own body, but the wife does. Do not deprive one another, except perhaps by agreement for a limited time, that you may devote yourselves to prayer; but then come together again, so that Satan may not tempt you because of your lack of self-control.

Isaiah 41:10

Fear not, for I am with you; be not dismayed, for I am your God; I will strengthen you, I will help you, I will uphold you with my righteous right hand.

1 Corinthians 7:26-28

I think that in view of the present distress it is good for a person to remain as he is. Are you bound to a wife? Do not seek to be free. Are you free from a wife? Do not seek a wife. But if you do marry, you have not sinned, and if a betrothed woman marries, she has not sinned. Yet those who marry will have worldly troubles, and I would spare you that.

1 Corinthians 7:2

But because of the temptation to sexual immorality, each man should have his own wife and each woman her own husband.

Matthew 19:12

For there are eunuchs who have been so from birth, and there are eunuchs who have been made eunuchs by men, and there are eunuchs who have made themselves eunuchs for the sake of the kingdom of heaven. Let the one who is able to receive this receive it."

Matthew 22:29-30

But Jesus answered them, "You are wrong, because you know neither the Scriptures nor the power of God. For in the resurrection they neither marry nor are given in marriage, but are like angels in heaven.

1 John 3:22

And whatever we ask we receive from him, because we keep his commandments and do what pleases him.

Matthew 19:4-6

He answered, "Have you not read that he who created them from the beginning made them male and female, and said, 'Therefore a man shall leave his father and his mother and hold fast to his wife, and the two shall become one flesh'? So they are no longer two but one flesh. What therefore God has joined together let not man separate."

Genesis 2:18

Then the Lord God said, "It is not good that the man should be alone; I will make him a helper fit for him."

Song of Solomon 3:5

I adjure you, O daughters of Jerusalem, by the gazelles or the does of the field, that you not stir up or awaken love until it pleases.

1 Corinthians 6:16

Or do you not know that he who is joined to a prostitute becomes one body with her? For, as it is written, "The two will become one flesh."

1 Corinthians 7:32

I want you to be free from anxieties. The unmarried man is anxious about the things of the Lord, how to please the Lord.

Matthew 6:33

But seek first the kingdom of God and his righteousness, and all these things will be added to you.

Isaiah 56:4-5

For thus says the Lord: "To the eunuchs who keep my Sabbaths, who choose the things that please me and hold fast my covenant, I will give in my house and within my walls a monument and a name better than sons and daughters; I will give them an everlasting name that shall not be cut off.

Jeremiah 29:11

For I know the plans I have for you, declares the Lord, plans for welfare and not for evil, to give you a future and a hope.

Isaiah 54:5

For your Maker is your husband, the Lord of hosts is his name; and the Holy One of Israel is your Redeemer, the God of the whole earth he is called.

Isaiah 34:16

Seek and read from the book of the Lord: Not one of these shall be missing; none shall be without her mate. For the mouth of the Lord has commanded, and his Spirit has gathered them.

1 Corinthians 7:26-40

I think that in view of the present distress it is good for a person to remain as he is. Are you bound to a wife? Do not seek to be free. Are you free from a wife? Do not seek a wife. But if you do marry, you have not sinned, and if a betrothed woman marries, she has not sinned. Yet those who marry will have worldly troubles, and I would spare you that. This is what I mean, brothers: the appointed time has grown very short. From now on, let those who have wives live as though they had none, and those who mourn as though they were not mourning, and those who rejoice as though they were not rejoicing, and those who buy as though they had no goods,

John 15:1-27

"I am the true vine, and my Father is the vinedresser. Every branch in me that does not bear fruit he takes away, and every branch that does bear fruit he prunes, that it may bear more fruit. Already you are clean because of the word that I have spoken to you. Abide in me, and I in you. As the branch cannot bear fruit by itself, unless it abides in the vine, neither can you, unless you abide in me. I am the vine; you are the branches. Whoever abides in me and I in him, he it is that bear much fruit, for apart from me you can do nothing.

Ruth 2:9

Let your eyes be on the field that they are reaping, and go after them. Have I not charged the young men not to touch you? And when you are thirsty, go to the vessels and drink what the young men have drawn."

Job 31:1-40

"I have made a covenant with my eyes; how then could I gaze at a virgin? What would be my portion from God above and my heritage from the Almighty on high? Is not calamity for the unrighteous, and disaster for the workers of iniquity? Does not he see my ways and number all my steps? "If I have walked with falsehood and my foot has hastened to deceit;

Proverbs 31:1-31

The words of King Lemuel, An oracle that his mother taught him: What are you doing, my son? What are you doing, son of my womb? What are you doing, son of my vows? Do not give your strength to women, your ways to those who destroy kings. It is not for kings, O Lemuel, it is not for kings to drink wine, or for rulers to take strong drink, lest they drink and forget what has been decreed and pervert the rights of all the afflicted.

Revelation 14:4

It is these who have not defiled themselves with women, for they are virgins. It is these who follow the Lamb wherever he goes. These have been redeemed from mankind as first fruits for God and the Lamb,

Romans 1:1-32

Paul, a servant of Christ Jesus, called to be an apostle, set apart for the gospel of God, which he promised beforehand through his prophets in the holy Scriptures, concerning his Son, who was descended from David according to the flesh and was declared to be the Son of God in power according to the Spirit of holiness by his resurrection from the dead, Jesus Christ our Lord, through whom we have received grace and apostleship to bring about the obedience of faith for the sake of his name among all the nations,

Job 31:1

"I have made a covenant with my eyes; how then could I gaze at a virgin?

About the Author

Jessica Davis is co-Pastor and co-Founder of Kingdom Seekers International Ministry of Arts, where she serves in ministry alongside her husband, Apostle Jonathan Davis. She is a native of West Memphis, Arkansas, where she is a proud wife and mother of two: Emmanuel and EnDyah (both coming soon). She is a woman whom God has graced and gifted with many different anointings, and she moves in them fluently and with excellence. She is an intercessor, mentor, praise and worship leader, and a mother to many. Jessica Davis is fueled by a passion to advance God's Kingdom, and to make His name praise in the earth. Known for her wit and sense of humor, she ministers effectively to the heart of God's people. She has a tender heart for single and married women alike. She desires women to break out of the box of limitations and expand their horizon to pursue purpose and destiny. She is valued for her wisdom and intellect, and her integrity is sound. Jessica Davis governs in the earth realm, and is determined to fulfill every prophetic word spoken over her life. Her desire is to carry out the spiritual mandate that God has placed in her hands.

To request Jessica Davis for speaking engagements and/or send a response or testimonies about this book, please email:

Kingdomseekers2011@att.net

or write

Attention: Jessica Davis

P.O. Box 1212

West Memphis, AR 72301

References

Quotes about Singleness

Hale, M. (n.d.). "The only thing worse than a boy who hates you: a boy that loves you.".*Quotes About Singleness (32 quotes)* http://www.goodreads.com/quotes/tag/singleness

31 Bible Verses about Singleness

31 Bible Verses about Singleness. (n.d.). *What Does the Bible Say About Singleness?* http://www.openbible.info/topics/singleness

Biblical References

Bible Gateway. (n.d.). *BibleGateway.com: A searchable online Bible in over 100 versions and 50 languages.*
http://www.biblegateway.com

Dictionary reference

http://www.dictionary.search.yahoo.com

Notes

Notes

www.ingramcontent.com/pod-product-compliance
Lightning Source LLC
Chambersburg PA
CBHW032215040426
42449CB00005B/607